POEMS by PAUL

all the best!

Paul Huggans

POEMS by PAUL

Simple But Deep

Paul Morgana RN.

To order additional copies of this book, contact:
Xlibris LLC
1-888-795-4274
www.Xlibris.com
Orders@Xlibris.com
132024

CONTENTS

Chapter 4 Historic Poems

Chapter 5 Patriotic Poems

Chapter 6 Fun Poems

Dina Morgana, her name is so sweet,
Was balancing me, when I first used my feet.

Keeping me warm, protecting my life,
Taught valuable lessons, "Don't run with that knife!"

Bandaged my knee, dried childhood tears,
When nightmares erupted, calmed all my fears.

Mom's advice as a teen, disregarded as foolish,
Heeding her words, would have made life less ghoulish.

Always in my corner, my biggest fan,
Shaped and molded me, into a responsible man.

Your voice has been silenced, I miss you the most,
With this dedication, your life I do toast!

CHAPTER 1
LOVE POEMS

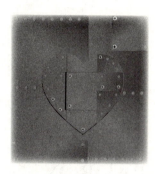

ARMOR

Her heart I'm told, is covered with steel,
A product she says, of many a raw deal.

So begins the process of starting to heal
Began already, we had our first meal.

As happiness begins, away with the steel
Love replaces metal, the heart again can feel.

Take care to those that melt free the heart,
If damaged again it may break apart.

BADBOY

What goes around, comes around, that's how it goes,
Sang the song many times, now my turn for the woes.

The woes I speak of, about a woman, she is oh so fair,
Powerful hands and fiery eyes, the great smell of her hair.

God keeps her away, as payment, for damaging other girls,
In younger days, I hurt them bad, twisting were their curls.

Now I have to pay a debt, for all the hurt and shame,
Payment comes at a high price, for these my stupid games.

This bad boy image served me well, I've had some good affair,
With many notches on my belt, who had the time to care?

But little did I know my love, the search was on for you,
I had some stops along the way, but nothing that was true.

It took many years of wondering, and finally you came,
Josephine is right for me, quite an amazing dame.

The only question for you god, an easy one you see,
How much more is owed to you before she'll be with me?

CONSUMED

What a find, lost my mind,
Found her on the net.
Looks were first, created a thirst,
A date was quickly set.

Food and drink, I caught a wink,
Cheers, to our first toast.
Our server knew, what she told us was true,
Told me I loved you the most.

A kiss she gave, it was all the rave,
Deep, passionate and hot.
I got a rise, the largest size,
Touching those lips hit the spot.

A never-ending date, we hardly did wait,
Lovemaking both day and night.
Opening your heart, not easy to start,
The closeness gave you a fright.

The months rolled by, never making me cry,
Tighter we grow by the hour.
Looking at your face, where you lay is my place,
My feelings will never get sour.

A ring made of gold, her finger I hold,
Consumed, I have lost all control.
Married today, forever I'll stay,
You own my heart and my soul!

DREAM

I had a dream the other night, guess who was the star?
Sitting in a smoke filled room, it was an old man's bar.

Drinking old man's drinks, the ones with scotch and rye,
What should I see that night, with my bloodshot eye?

A beautiful girl appeared, and clinging to her thighs,
This skintight dress made all of silk, designed in just your size.

In her hand she had a smoke, and blew some in my face,
I tried to snatch the dress in back, but couldn't grab the lace.

Coughing and choking I looked at her, as she walked away,
I got excited watching her walk; her hips did dip and sway.

By now it's pretty obvious, member hard in my pants,
Walked right up behind her and asked, honey do you dance?

When finally I saw her face, much to my surprise,
Guess who was starring back at me, I wouldn't tell you lies.

My beautiful Josephine was looking in my eyes,
Silky blonde hair on her head, that dress that grabbed her thighs.

She said, hey baby I'm standing here, will it take all night,
For you to come and kiss my lips, and try to get it right.

I laid my lips across her face and got a big wet kiss,
Suddenly my dream was done; I wake in the abyss.

Looking at the night table, what there should I find?
An ashtray with some stale smoked butts, happened to be your kind.

I got right there out of bed, and on something I slip,
The hot silk dress I dreamed about, that clinged all to your hip.

Upon hitting the floor and banging my head, I heard a soft low voice,
Are you ok? She said to me, to answer I had no choice.

I'm ok love of mine, I'll come right back to bed,
When finally getting close to her, I kissed her on the head.

Was it real or did I dream, what difference does it make,
My loves warm body next to mine, her heart is what I take.

FACE

We met by fates hand,
In a cruel and harsh place,

Death and disease abound,
Then the sight of your face.

Betrayal and backstabbing
Is common in this place,

And then I saw it,
Your beautiful face.

Through the bosses and soldiers
That have fallen from grace,

That's when I saw it . . . .
Your beautiful face.

A place of comfort and healing
No this is not the case,

Then the sun shone brightly . . . .
And I saw your face.

Why are people so cruel,
They must always win the race,

That matters little to me,
So long as I see your face.

FRENZY

My red hot passion over the top it boils,
Our bodies entwined, like DNA coils.

Can't tell where I left off, and you begin,
Loving you so, the world it does win.

Makes us better to our fellow man,
Helps me to be the best that I can.

Loving you makes me soar above,
Take flight on the back of a winged dove.

Touch you again, your heart burning with fire,
Desire uncontrolled, reaching higher and higher!

Sweating and dripping, the sheets are a mess,
Still half on your beautiful, silk laden dress.

I love the feel of the dress on your skin,
Consuming my soul, I'm placing it in.

Frenzied love making, my ardor it burned,
Around the bed, new moves I have learned.

Finally placed you under my spell,
Your spasming body, turned into gel.

The madness is passing, get closer and hold,
Give me you body, your sole you have sold,

I have the contract, you've signed on the line,
Let's have another go, I'll make you feel fine!

KISS

Humans have a special way to show emotional bliss,
I've gotten some, and given some, can you guess what's this?

They mean much to women, their liked by men as well,
To coin a phrase, getting one can really ring your bell.

A candy has the name, I speak of in this rhyme,
Made of chocolate, wrapped in foil, eaten all the time.

Kisses have been around, since man lived in the cave,
Maybe even before then, there really quite the rave!

From early as an infant, moms kisses were all mine.
To celebrate a special time, or sooth me when I'd whine.

The first girl my own age, to kiss me on the face,
We shared a sir name, and address, the kitchen was the place.

Oh Dear! She would say to me, in her funny voice,
We'd watch the tube, and laugh a lot, there was no other choice.

My sister is the girl I speak of, I love her to this day,
We've shared many a good time, still love to laugh and play!

The first non-family female, who shared a kiss with me,
Her name was Sue, not one or two, but kisses totaled three.

There are many kinds of kisses, ones meant to heal,
Usually given by a mom, no cures but better you feel.

Or kisses for the passion, they prelude a sensuous folly,
Deep and wet, your soul ablaze, this time her name was Molly.

A common way for women, to greet a friendly face,
A cheek is where it lands, the only acceptable place.

The air kiss has been gaining steam, with the jet set crowd,
No touching of body parts is condoned or is allowed.

The people of Eastern Europe have a strange way to kiss,
Both cheeks a man is pecked upon, the firing squad won't miss.

Called the Russian "kiss of death", may follow a long ride,
Siberian terrain legend says, many a body does it hide.

The Middle East kissing, may be hard to complete,
All wrapped in veils, don't look at her, her family on you may beat,

So therapeutic, passionate or given to a foe,
The kiss has many twists and turns, its meaning we never know.

LEAVING

She's sure its the right thing,
Too fast my love embracing.

She sends me out into the night,
The very thought gives me fright.

She says leave, I have another,
Didn't know who, maybe my brother.

He's a man from the past, with nary a chance,
To wine and dine me, and make romance.

She's dealt me a fatal crushing blow,
No idea what to do, or where to go.

Hard now to breath or think or move,
No more will we talk or laugh or groove.

My life now is finished, over and done,
No more lover or friend or fun.

No reason to continue, go on why,
The one I long for is not being shy.

With her new found love, kissing and holding,
I'm sure by now their bodies are molding.

Its time now to end, this broken life's story,
With a long messy fall, it will be gory

Is that one high enough? Don't know for sure,
My thoughts not for church, are totally impure.

I get to the top, and God calls my name,
Jump he says, I will not take the blame.

Was it god or the devil talking the word,
Forty stories I had fallen when I suddenly heard,

My loves voice crying broken and sad,
Paul please come back, I miss you so bad.

MARRIED

The comfort and passion that I have found,
Makes little sense, feet still off the ground.

You changed my mind, I know not why,
Just in time, I wanted to die.

Without you here, things weren't the same,
I'd go through the motions, it was all pretty lame.

Were back and beyond, our first time around,
Planning a vacation, Villa Roma you've found.

Meeting your family, dad wants to know,
Better love my girl, she isn't a hoe.

All this drama, I do take it well,
I look at your face, it's easy to sell.

Cause I'm buying a family, including your kids,
I want to love all, they'll be flipping their lids,

When we tell them our plans, to become man and wife,
I promise to love them, the rest of their life.

It matters not, where the living takes place,
All I need, is the sight of your face.

New memories, we will make, day by day,
Love keeps growing, finally I say,

Marriage is good, and my life it is rich,
Never thought again, I would get hitched.

The lord he smiles, and blesses our time,
Peaceful and easy, I'll continue to rhyme.

RANDOM

We met by chance in the liquor store,
Stretching for cigars, your scent was pure.

A smile flashed my eyes, teeth white as snow,
Met at checkout time, more about you I would know.

A big party at your house tonight,
Hoping its a hit, you had a little fright.

A box of Monticristos, more info she did give,
Come and join in, she told me where she lived.

Not the type to turn down this fun,
I told her yes, then she had to run.

Tonight is casual dress, festivities at eight,
I said, "Thanks", the party will be great!

Primed and prodded, cleaned up nice,
Then brushed my teeth, I did it twice.

I rang the bell, I caught her smell,
The same scent as before.
I could tell, the party was swell,
It ended at a quarter to four.

The party was done, but the real fun,
Started when cleanup was through.
You're looking fine, upon you I'll dine,
Better I want to know you.

She said come to bed, her clothes she did shed,
I couldn't resist all her charms.
A bottle of Moet, we hadn't touched yet,
She fell asleep in my arms.

Woke together in the morning she said to me bye,
Soft voice cracked, with a tear drop in her eye.

Thanks for staying, but time now to go,
My husband is coming, time for the show.

SEDUCTION

From the moment I saw her beautiful face,
For me there was no other place,

Across the table, I moved with haste,
So of her lips, I'd get a taste.

The hair was soft like fresh spun silk,
And skin as smooth as mothers milk.

The eyes so dark, bedroom brown,
Nothing about her made me frown.

Lips softer than the pedal of a rose,
Prissy and pouting and striking a pose.

Skin so firm and filled with vigor,
Cannot resist so I pulled the trigger.

I asked her please to take me home,
I need to kiss and touch and roam.

Your wondrous shape that makes quiver,
Ok, said she, some cake for you, only a sliver.

I knew that her taste would surely please,
Its brought me down to my knees.

Seduction is strong and I can't resist,
The touch of her hand and the feel of her wrist.

A strong girl is she, energy abounds,
Commands me to lick her sweet pubic mounds.

Passion subsides, now its just us two,
Your mind still tells, me what to do.

I must obey; your in total control,
Seduction has stolen my very soul.

SEEMS

The wonder and excitement, like living dreams,
Life is not always as it seems.

The pain and suffering and love lost,
Has come to her at a terrible cost.

So desire and pleasure and corporal fun,
Replaces the need to be with just one.

E-mails, chat rooms and serial dating,
Have replaced the desire for serious mating.

Then along come I, who will turn it around,
No more love lost, eternally bound.

Talking and holding, understanding her head,
Passionate kissing and going to bed.

Who am I you say, to change this life,
The one who cares enough to make her my wife.

SEX

We met on a Monday, and little did I know,
This irresistible creature, whose name was Jo,

Would arouse and tempt me, and completely tease,
Bringing me down, to my knees.

Like a fool I thought, "this can't be real"
Her hand and touch, I love to feel.

Her passionate kisses, like never before,
Have left me breathless and begging for more.

Her body is long, lean and craves touch
I'm loosing myself, I like it too much.

Naked and sweating and grinding and sucking,
The smell of her hair, and the sound of our fucking,

Leaves me clamoring, choking and wanting some more.
I feel like a junkie and so need to score.

Her body tender, supple and sweet,
I love when she rubs me, soft with her feet.

We are never done love making, here's a clue why,
When I go out of arms reach or look at her eye.

I know to not please her, will make her cry,
I run the risk of loosing her, and surely will die.

SIZZLE

Look at her body, take in the face,
Both of these items lead me to grace.

Starting with a very tiny glance,
I feel a stirring deep in my pants.

Then a smile, with her pearly whites,
The sight of her legs in shapely tights.

Loves to shake it, I dig watching her move,
Exciting and viral, getting on my groove.

A silky hot blouse clings to those curves.
Can't resist how it moves, when her body it swerves.

Letting down that hair, shiny and free,
Comes all the way down, way below her knee.

Twisting her head, watch the locks fly,
Stops for a movement, peers into your eye,

She's ready, this feeling you can't buy,
Her body on fire and let's out a sigh,

Like an Indian warrior, ready to fight,
Our lovemaking slightly resembles this sight.

First a tender deep reaching kiss,
Her tongue it surrounds me, like a snake it does hiss.

Soft caressing, gentle but firm,
Soon her body begins to wriggle and squirm.

My hand I use to slap on her tush,
So firm and hard, never like mush.

Her bottom hot and red as a beet,
I think she's ready, again our lips meet.

Passionate movement our bodies are swirling,
Climaxing, I see her toes they are curling.

A five minute break and were at it once more,
Can't resist her charms, I'm ready to score!

SLAVE

You walked past, it was the last,
A free man I am not.
Flowing hair, touch it I dare,
My body is flaming hot.

Thinking of you, is all I do,
They have a term, a slave.
Waiting for your call, I need to maul,
With you I need not behave.

Who is your man, your biggest fan,
Completely under you spell,
Feeling weak, I need you to speak,
One word from you and I'm well.

Enough with talk, don't make me stalk,
Come tell me I'm the one.
I'll give my all, won't let you fall,
With me always having fun.

The days roll by, never more do I sigh,
My heart you hold in your hand.
Never do I preach, I implore and beseech
Be my wife and your life will be grand

Place on your hand, a golden band,
A couple forever more.
Love I give, all the days that I live,
Your slave whether man rich or poor.

SMITTEN

Hi my girl, thoughts do swirl,
Under your beautiful hair.
Answer the phone, tonight I'm alone,
Show me a sign that you care.

I look in your eyes, knowing you're wise,
Smitten is my loved starved heart.
Feeling your fright, it's only one night,
This relation, to fast it does start.

Blame it on me, never more can I be,
With anyone other than you.
Where my eyes I place, I see your face,
I know my feelings are true.

The story by Bill, always give me a chill,
Romeo fell hard in one night.
Give me your mind, with it I'm kind,
Once dull, now the future is bright.

Last night I brought fear, too perfect when near,
No longer could you stay in my arms.
A tear in your eye, too slow to dry,
What's happening? Can't resist all these charms.

Walk with me in life, you'll be a good wife,
Never been surer than now,
Kiss my lips, your love has grips,
On my soul, I never ask how.

SUBMIT

The weather was cold, the wind did howl,
Faces in the street wearing only a scowl.

Presidents day, a date with a girl,
When talking on the phone, my head did swirl.

Let's go back, another week,
We met on line, yet to speak.

Her profile and a picture popped up on my screen,
I never hit enter, she was tall and lean.

Her aura it grabbed me, enslaving my soul,
My fingers start typing, I lost their control.

Sending her pleasantries, we found common ground,
I dialed the number, and was digging her sound.

We talked and went on for hours, a style uncommon to me,
Finally I said, you make me laugh, let's have coffee or tea?

The date was on, I'm feeling strong,
A dinner in her hometown.
Parked my car, sat at the bar, and ordered a drink that was brown.

Suddenly turned, quickly I learned,
I love the smell of her hair.
Standing at my side, I almost died,
Nothing else in the world did I care.

Taking a chance, I asked her to dance,
She kissed me and flipped out my lid!
Making love until dawn, soon we would spawn,
A bundle, most call them a kid.

Still love her today, bedroom games we do play,
Children, the number is three,
While professing her love, I'm transported above,
My eyes get wet, I can't see.

TOGETHER

I sit and wait for your return,
Feeling good, muscles burn.

My life with you is rising high,
We talk and laugh, I touch the sky.

Things improve, better each day,
Into your heart, I found a way.

Acceptance both, for what we are,
Not malicious, negativity we bar.

I do things, to make you proud,
Your name I call, and say it loud.

Josephine is the one I adore,
Can't get enough, always wanting more.

Your smile, your wit, to look at your face,
I see in her eyes, she wants to share space.

But first things first, and day by day,
Love grows up high, and finds a way.

To keep her close, my arms around,
Her muscular shoulders, so glad I found,

The one I yearn for, she fills my soul,
With love and affection, once an empty hole.

She tells me tonight, let's share our life,
Maybe soon, I'll be your wife.

So another night together, fun is in store.
Right off the train, come open my door.

I'll give you a ride, right into the house,
Never again, you'll deal with a louse.

Shopping and laughing, perfect we fit,
Tonight in our bed, while swapping spit,
And making love, and sharing wit,
I'll profess my love, the fire you've lit.

The best thing is, that at days end,
I know tomorrow, we do it again.

God is good, time he has lent,
For me and my girl, good feelings he's sent.

The cycle complete, she gave me a key,
The journey continues, a couple we be.

TURN

Please my sweet baby, don't turn your back,
Time won't change, in a relationship what lacks.

All the others, they had their time,
To drop everything, and wine and dine.

And turn your head and make think,
You couldn't live, without their wink.

Can't turn back the clock, and bodies be young,
Keeping things fresh, the songs I have sung.

I come to you, with one thought in mind,
Keeping you happy 'till the end of time.

Loving, hugging and many a night,
In the throws of passion, never a fight.

Many have tried, and many have failed,
You can see there faces, many have bailed.

Trying to win your sweet loving heart,
To many, you gave them, not even a part.

Trying to keep hearts armor bound,
Dumping men hard with nary a sound.

Its my turn now, to make you my own,
Talking for hours, over the phone.

Making plans and getting to know,
The wondrous things, that make our love grow.

Please my sweet love, embrace what I'm giving,
My heart and my soul poured into our living.

Its my turn now to sweep you off your feet,
Another like me, you may never meet.

UNSTOPPABLE

Dearest lover and still my friend,
No bounds it knows, to never end.

These feelings run deep, sounding cliché',
Love knows no end, it shows us the way.

Bodies apart is the reality today,
Another to tame, your words do say.

Only the miles keep us apart,
Still I reside deep in your heart.

Mask the feelings, so none can see,
Even from yourself, hide them from me.

There will come a day, down the road,
Feelings come alive, and suddenly explode.

My sweet young love, rush to my arms,
Never again will I resist all your charms.

Years I have wasted, are your feelings alive?
Now I can love you, together we'll thrive.

This may take some time, it matters not,
If not in this lifetime, many I've got.

I will wait for you, love knows no end,
My heart and my soul, to you I do send.

WIFE

Sleep in the dark, think of the park,
The first place we were together.
A frenzied scene, your bottom is green,
The mood light as a feather.

On a blanket we lay, exhausted by play,
Watched the rising sun,
Had so much fun, let's have another run,
For breakfast a cinnamon bun.

After breakfast we walk, we listen, we talk,
Sharing both conquest and strife,
I look in your eyes, I know its not wise,
I ask you to be my wife.

Years go round, never a sound,
Of discontent, or a hint of the blues,
Anniversary cake, special she'd bake.
I need to tell you some news.

I started to shake, didn't know what to make,
Her face with a terrible look.
I'm leaving you dear, don't shed a tear,
Life is stolen by a terrible crook.

What is the reason, to leave me this season,
Why now are we through?
I'm sick and may die, please dry your eye,
Its cancer that's making me blue.

Fought a great fight, doctors cant make it right,
I hear acceptance in her voice
Bedridden and weak, hardly could speak,
Be happy my love that's my choice.

She left that day, nothing else to say,
Empty now is my life.
Lays in the ground, not making a sound,
Oh God, how I miss my wife!

WOW

Getting ready for our date, a suit and tie affair,
I just take a shower and drag a comb through my hair.

For her its not so easy, beginning around four,
Hard pressed we will be, to walk out of the door.

A forty-minute shower, "I have to shave my legs,"
Never leaves a drop of hot water, for this, my body begs.

Towel dry, pile lotion high,
Rub deep in your skin,
Your smelling good, I knew you would,
Its me that's going to win.

Next the wild dew, she must try and tame,
Curling iron used, she's a master at this game.

The focus next, the eyes we'll test,
Stretch the lashes long,
Mascara and the liner, she's looking finer,
The whole time humming a song.

The bathroom's mine, of this she'll whine,
Don't want to see her less,
The next is the best, beats all the rest
Painting on her beautiful dress!

I shower and shave, come out unscathed,
Get dressed with blinding speed,
She's had a while, to build up her style,
Can't wait to dance, I will lead.

Waiting by the door, her beauty does pour,
Out for all to see.
"Wow!" I say, looking great today,
Can't believe she is for me!

CHAPTER 2
FAMILY POEMS

MOM

Hi mom, I've been thinking of you, hoping all is well,
Gone and missed are you, many days have been hell.

I have many questions unanswered by you,
What caused your anger, why were you so blue?

Why were your messages, encased in meanings double,
It caused me much confusion, and got me in some trouble.

Children need stability, consistency a must,
Your teachings made it difficult, to love need and trust.

The anger and the hatred, carried in your heart,
Continues to destroy your family, ripping us apart.

Yelling was your way, to discipline your child;
Personality was harsh, nothing about you was mild.

A great mom were you, when we were young and weak,
Once decisions we need make, you wouldn't let us speak.

Cooking and cleaning these things were done with ease,
But emotions deep within our hearts never did you appease.

Children love their parents, its inherent to the breed,
But parents can be toxic, not meeting emotional need.

I know there was a trauma, in your life as a girl,
When I think about it my head begins to swirl.

I love and miss you mom, this I promise twice,
I only wish your parenting didn't have such a high price.

DAD

Born in Brooklyn, you had a tough start,
Foster care and abuse, family torn apart.

Your mother would abandon you, unstable was she,
Your father was evil, what kind of man would you be?

Living with families that didn't really care,
Dollars for them, nothing for you to wear,

A weak bladder caused bathtub sleeping at three,
Monsters they were spawning, didn't anyone see?

The Catania's came, and life turned around,
Food and heat, you were suddenly found.

Happy were you, reunited with your sister,
After years of neglect, a band aid for the blister.

Suddenly life again upside down,
Father was back, with a vicious frown.

He came to New York and yanked you and your sis,
Out of Catania's, sweet loving bliss.

A cold water flat, with little to eat,
Lucky, a neighbor on you she was sweet.

Carrying laundry in Brooklyn's rough street,
A little money, for anything to eat.

Play ball with friends, surely get beat,
The old man wanted you home at his feet.

A neighbor could no longer take all the noise,
Child services came and to you they were poised,

To liberate and set you free,
And be all the man you could be.

DAUGHTER

Passion ignited with a man and his wife,
After the fire ebbs, begins a new life.

Grows and expands, please mom take care,
Give baby a chance, no smoking, be fair.

Take your vitamins, eating do right,
Keep doctors appointments, lessen your plight.

A sonograms taken, babies picture, a first,
Smile for the camera, a sudden movement burst.

It must be a girl, she posed for the shot,
Even in utero, she wants to look hot.

Continues to increase in shape and in size,
Parents ask questions, of people more wise.

Hoping for knowledge, to gain and to use,
Avoiding mistakes, and sidestepping the blues.

Finally comes the day she is born,
Dilated fully, placenta is torn.

Cleaned and warned, you finally hold,
Your daughter is healthy, is what you are told.

The first second she is placed in your arm,
Controlling your mind, is to stop her from harm.

When is her first tooth to be cut?
Will she be happy, keep food in her gut.

Is dance class today, what time does it start?
She just smiled at you, this tugs on your heart!

Life with your daughter, you never would sell,
You'd die to protect her, the family as well.

Priceless is her site, and hearing this sound,
I love you daddy! Good feelings abound.

SON

The object of every father's desire,
Making him an athlete, is what you aspire.

Wean him on sports, teach him all that you know,
Go to his games, watching the show.

Set a good example, staying in shape,
Never letting him know, you don't wear a cape.

He looks up to you, as though you're a god,
In reality, closer you may be to a clod.

This matters not, his respect you will gain,
To accomplish this feat may bring you some pain.

The discomfort is both from financial and muscle,
Pay for his sports, and with him you will rustle.

Coming home from work, hot and tired,
Catching his fastball, you're totally wired.

The time may come when he needs to quit,
Giving up on the dream, love him more than a bit.

Disappointment for both, your son will be sad,
Thinks he's a failure, and at him you're mad.

Please make it clear, explain with a grin,
You couldn't be prouder, of where he has been.

Your life has just started, my son you do be,
Couldn't care for you more, I want you to see.

Sports no longer matter, just be a good man,
Mom and I love you, do all that you can,

To make the world, a better place to live,
One hundred percent is what you must give.

ROADS

Which road to take is always a mystery,
A problem many times seen in history.

The straight and narrow, leads the way,
Sometimes we get sidetracked, by love or by play.

What starts out the right road, you begin to walk,
End up with stories, about which you can't talk.

There comes to all a fork in the road,
Not a kitchen utensil, a different life you are showed.

One path may lead to fortune and fame,
The other has shame disgrace and to blame.

Did I chose the right path, will I be a success?
Or does this path leave my life in a mess?

I think a fork is always a good thing,
Take a chance, never know what it'll bring.

If the path you've taken is not your desire,
Find another path, you will light it on fire!

The person makes their own way in life,
Not a mother, brother, friend or your wife.

Any path taken leads to good things,
Passion and commitment will give you wings.

They will take to places you see in your dream,
Live out your fantasies, just as they seem.

Hard work, passion and dedication you'll find,
Bring all good things, what do you have in mind?

GOD

Immortal life span, cannot conceive,
His own beginning, the Eons he does weave.

Not only Earth, many other worlds to guide,
How does he do it, in his shoes I want to ride.

If the subject of what I speak,
A mystery resolved, your interest I will peak.

God is the subject, many ponder his thought.
Help from him, many more are sought.

His justice and wisdom unmatched by man,
Forgive and understand, sin whenever we can.

Not like we try, just a natural thing,
Envy and greed and lusting they bring,

What God himself placed in our soul,
He understands when people loose control.

Committing unmerciful acts against those,
You should be embracing, that's what god has chose.

He gave his son, and what did we do?
Nailed to a cross, mankind soon would rue,

The decision to crucify gods begotten son,
To make him a king, is what we should have done.

God knew what would happen, still he would send,
Jesus to the world, but politicians wouldn't bend.

Still forgiven are those sending him to demise,
All knowing and powerful, totally wise.

Blind faith is needed, to believe in his work,
Jump on his wagon, make haste and don't shirk!

NOURISHMENT

The world is a cold and exacting place,
Filled with animals, on land and in space.

Most of these creatures kill to survive,
Stalking is needed, to live and to thrive.

Lions pursue antelope, wolves hunt rabbit,
Vestige is basic, killing is a habit.

What of the race, with the most brain power,
Slaughtering helpless animals, my mouth tasting sour.

This was an acceptable way to eat,
In the distant past, wild animals provide meat.

But raising chickens, pigs and cattle,
For easy termination, makes my teeth rattle.

There are more proficient ways for man to get food,
Than breeding livestock, this method is crude.

Vegetables and dairy, legumes do provide,
The proteins needed to keep people alive.

All living creatures deserve a fighting chance,
Become a vegetarian, take a humane stance.

Your health will improve, pounds will be shed,
Increase in energy, less time spent in bed.

Life span increases, disease on the run,
Killing innocent animals is no longer done.

COURT

Child support is finally going to end,
For those just starting, a message I send.

My time in court was wasted life,
Never able to completely divorce my wife.

Scorned and upset by my marital decision,
She wants to challenge my fatherly position.

A lawyer retained with earnings I made,
Our houses equity, she was to raid.

Lies and claims, falling not on deaf ears,
To visit with my child, took many years.

Brainwashing my daughter, never a hug,
You would think, I'm a murderous thug.

Support was ordered, a sizable amount,
Behind on the rent, not enough money to count.

Motions and orders, she continued to file,
Poorer was I, while she lived in style.

The day arrived, emancipation was near,
The final court date, still at me she does leer.

My female judge had no recourse,
Chains were removed, now I feel the divorce.

Freedom at last, I'm no longer a slave,
Money in the bank, I can finally save.

I hope you were listening, this message is dear,
Avoid going to court, of its doors stay clear.

HEALTH

Watch your weight, limit the salt,
If my eating is poor, it's not my fault.

Pasta and cheese, a meat laden dish,
Comfort found in food, lasagna is my wish.

My Italian parents helped feed me well,
Now as an adult, I'm going through hell.

I still fill my mouth, as I did when a youth,
Pant sizes increasing is the only real truth.

Suck in that gut, on your bed do the worm,
Into those blue jeans, your trying to squirm.

Blood pressure and cholesterol on a serious rise,
Easy it is to believe my own lies.

"Your not fat, you wear it so fine,"
On too many meals, I'm wanting to dine.

I'm not alone, our country is a mess,
Obesity is rising, so is our stress.

Its never too late, for turning life around,
Instead of that snack, let those feet hit the ground.

You don't need to be Arnold, small changes will work,
Walk up those stairs, the yard work don't shirk.

Get an exercise partner, to help motivate your head,
Drop off some carbs, one less slice of bread.

Swimming is good, it's easy on the joints,
When feeling younger, up your member it points.

Calories burn making love, now your women is happy,
There's no going back, to feeling so crappy.

Being more fit, will increase your net worth,
The food bill is down, and so is your girth,

Less is more, is my motto this day,
More fun awaits, the less you weigh!

BUSINESS

Poetry I create, this doesn't rate,
Need to learn to sell.
My stuff they like, during open mic,
The marketing is hell!

New to this, don't want to miss,
The opportunity great,
Business needs, are difficult deeds,
I find it hard to wait.

Time it taketh, a website to maketh,
A hundred things to choose,
Emails are plenty, phone calls are many,
Selling my creation, I can't snooze.

So hears the deal, I'm getting real,
Marketing I will learn,
Offers red, until eyes bled,
Candle at both ends I burn.

A publicist retained, never I complained,
10% they have earned,
Some pressure lost, its worth the cost,
Stomach no longer churned.

Corrections to make, I cannot fake,
A slow and arduous trip.

Driving is how, I get there now,
Creation time I must skip.

So here we go, not laying low,
Published is the book,
Off to signing, never whining,
The crowds I cannot look.

Tired am I, sometimes cry,
Lonesome on the road,
I miss my home, don't want to roam,
Still not in writing mode.

Groupies are near, I always hear,
"Please Paul read some work."
This makes me blue, I must be true,
Can't appear a jerk.

This newfound fame, I play the game,
Recognized where I trot,
Can overwhelm, I loose the helm,
I need a quiet spot.

Don't misunderstand, I think it's grand,
My newfound wealth and fame,
Just need to pace, to win the race,
And learn to play the game.

EYES

The emotions of man are easy to read,
They glisten and shine, never a need,

To ask your friend, how does he feel,
I'll give you a clue, here's how you steal,

And know exactly, what's in his head,
Can't hide it from you, until he is dead.

Don't need to be Bond, a secret service spy,
Just get close to his face, peer into his eye.

The eyes are the windows to the soul,
See tempers get hot, and you may loose control.

Sadness is seen, clear as the sky,
The loss of a loved one, why now did they die?

Happiness comes as the eye starts to glean,
No mistaking the look of it, can't miss its sheen.

Anger it rages, the eye may turn red,
Body language will show, what lurks in their head.

Love is another, not easy to miss,
May lean close to you, and give you a kiss.

Some of these emotions will mix in your eye,
Like happiness and love, it may make you cry.

Sadness and anger, may travel in sync,
You'll see them at bars, pounding a drink.

A student of man, I always do look,
At a persons eyes, can read like a book.

People will try and hide how they feel,
I look at those pupils, and I know what is real.

You may ask yourself what's the purpose of this?
Prying into emotions, can make some folks hiss.

I like the plain truth, found in the eye,
Can't be lied to, I never ask why?

FRIEND

In younger days, of long ago,
Many a man, that I called bro.

As time went by, and I lost touch,
The ones I kept, I value much.

In youth it seems that making ties,
Was easily done, with many guys.

School was the place, to socialize,
Your choice of friends, not always wise.

The student body, choices abound,
Any number of friends, could be found.

As children both thoughts and goals,
Were all the same, football between the poles.

Or get on base, and touch the plate,
Getting anxiety, over your first date.

But youth it faded, into the past,
And many friendships, wouldn't last.

Off to college and quickly loose touch,
With people that one time, meant so much.

New people we meet, in work or at school,
Some got close, others make you the fool.

Now all grown up, and your circle of friends,
Grows smaller and thinner, without any ends.

Buddies you've left, are just memories today,
Some raised a family, or moved away.

Others lived their lives, and then you hear,
Poor Jim got cancer, passed away last year.

Sam was driving, impaired one night,
A terrible accident, it caused me fright.

I have a friend, from younger days,
He's changed much, in many ways.

Still many a thread, that ties us together,
After speaking with him, mood light as a feather.

Endorphins and memories, he doth stir,
Of younger days, and the way we were.

I go all out, to stay close with him,
Calling often, even on a whim,

Telling him how much, he means to me,
And making plans, for him to see,

My new 5 iron, its a real prize,
I see it when I look at his eyes.

He cherishes my company and the time,
We spend together, stop on a dime,

If a problem arises, and he needs an ear,
To listen and aid, his issue I hear.

So the moral of my story told,
When it comes to friendship, effort be bold,

To keep your friends, stay forever in touch,
Only once their gone, will you miss them so much.

CHAPTER 3
NATURE POEMS

WINTER

Wow, the weather sure is cold,
Days are short, the wind is bold.

The season isn't a favorite for sure,
Most in the cold, aren't begging for more.

This testament to the winter, is short and is sweet,
Its brutal cold, upon you does beat.

And beg for spring, and longer days,
And new found fun in different ways.

But back to winter, now let's explore,
Its wondrous beauty, many do adore,

The frosty nights, a blanket of snow,
Untouched and virgin, a skiing we can go!

Take the kids to the local park,
Sleigh ride with them, a youthful spark,

May be rekindled, inside your soul,
This surely is fun, never is it droll.

Build a snowman, with coal and pipe,
He may come alive, frosty isn't just hype.

The alive that he comes, is not in the snow,
But in the hearts of the ones that help make him grow.

Spending time with the family, this bonding is good,
Feeling alive and well, with your family you should,

The wondrous winter, has the holiest of days,
A time to be kind, and have gentler ways.

The birth of the savior, the greatest of men,
His spirit reborn, and we all know when,

This holiday comes, its time be kind,
Good deeds and good thoughts, cover your mind.

The new year comes in winter, a time to start new,
Cast aside bad habits, and with them your through.

Good cheer and good times, and drinking some wine,
Kissing and hugging, and playing Auld Lang Syne.

Presidents day is a time to give thanks,
Lincoln and the north, and the fighting yanks,

Put an end to slavery, blacks are free as whites,
Another century passed to gain civil rights.

Praise to Washington, the first to lead,
Our country from Britain, his troops had freed,

The people of the Colonies, America was born,
Plains full of plenty, many acres of corn.

Valentines day, the time for romance,
Put yourself out there, ask a girl to a dance!

The celebration turns history around,
Originally on this day, many bodies were found,

Dead in a garage, in the Chicago town,
The pictures are gruesome, bloodstains on the ground.

These are the times in winters' cold,
That have special meaning, and memories they hold.

Look kindly on winter, its end will bring,
A time of rebirth known as spring.

SPRING

The calendar reads March the winter is done,
Its time for the spring and all kinds of fun!

Work your body, as the days grow long,
Exercise your muscles, and get real strong!

Things come alive trees start to bud,
Testosterone flows, men feel like a stud.

Women look for a man to provide,
Less clothes on the body, no skin to hide

Play ball! The baseball umpires cry,
A long fly ball, hit high into the sky.

Unstable weather, warm and then cold,
It matters little, this story is told,

About the season that is loved by most,
The days lengthen, and other things to boast,

Like the hockey playoffs, at Madison Square,
Turn on the TV and pull up a chair,

Watch the Rangers play and kick some tail,
When shooting the puck, they cannot fail.

Easter time occurs in the spring,
The son of God and strong feelings he brings,

The story does tell, of his death on the cross,
Mankind's big mistake, what a terrible loss.

All these good things, happen in the spring,
Nature smiles at this time, and we fly on her wing.

SUMMER

The weather is hot, inside your not,
Winter is no more.
Days are long, you're feeling strong,
Fun you have in store.

The A/C on, when you're gone,
Electric bills do rise.
Turn off the juice, start cutting loose,
Outside there are blue skies.

The days are long, come sing a song,
At last the summers here,
Clean up the porch, light a torch,
And have ourselves a beer!

Let's hit the beach, and we can reach,
Our skin a golden hue,
Dig in the sand, with my bare hand,
Rainy days I am blue.

Biking in the park, we'll have a lark,
Riding here and there,
Meeting friends, it all depends,
Which direction you do bare.

Look to the right, he's flying a kite,
A friend from years gone past.
Summer is best, giving you zest,
Reminisce and have a blast!

Let's hit the links, your swing it stinks,
Your buddy doesn't care,
That one fine shot, will hit the spot,
A good time you will share.

Out on a boat, around we'll float,
Let's cast our poles and wait,
Your line is taught, I think you caught,
The big one's on your plate.

Concerts in the park, start after dark,
Bring your favorite date,
Hear the sounds, good mood abounds,
Romance it does await.

Not all fun, work must get done,
The yard it begs for time,
Needs some seed, water and weed,
Fertilize and lime.

Cut and rake, your back will ache,
Stop to have some lunch,
Work is done, time for fun,
Invite friends, let's have brunch.

Baseball season, is the reason,
Some couples get a divorce,
Games every night, causing plight,
Loneliness is the source.

At summers end, this message I send,
The season hurry back,
Winter, spring and fall, keep them all
Next to summer they do lack.

FALL

The weather is hot, your spirit is weak,
Then enter fall, its what you seek.

In early fall, the days stay long,
The nights are crisp, please sing my song.

And tell the world, about the wonders of fall,
Text a friend, or give them a call!

The world series is played in the fall,
Let's hope the Yankees win it all!

And speaking of sports, its time for the clash,
Of helmets and pads, and a 40 yard dash.

Footballs will fly, and then Eli has poise,
To hoist the Lombardi, and make some loud noise.

Open the windows the cool breeze blows,
No A/C needed, no electricity woes.

Let's carve a pumpkin, and rake the yard,
And wear a costume, its not very hard.

To trick or treat, and act real silly,
A scary outfit, may give you the willies.

We can go for a ride and see a great view,
The reds and gold's, an amazing hue.

Of tree sap running, the leaves they do change,
Once green as a dollar, to an earth tone range.

An American holiday is at falls end,
Celebrate pilgrim success, and the message it sends.

To give thanks to your maker, for the gifts he bestow,
And toast to the season, don't be late! Off you go!

To visit some family, eats and treats,
Pies and cakes, and a variety of meats.

Leftovers for days, loosen your belt,
You need the stair master, to again be svelte.

The final days of the season are cold,
The days are short, the weather is bold.

We Christians wait for the holy day,
The savor is coming, the next season they say,

Is the time for rejoicing, and spreading the word,
Jesus is born again, his story is heard,

In the poem about winter, you'll just have to wait,
Its no loose reading for you and your mate.

CLOUDS

Head up when your feeling low,
Look up high, and watch the show.

The show I speak of, occurs all day,
Whether sunny or not, never need to pay,

A fee to watch, no actors to play,
The parts I speak of, nature's way.

Floating far, above the earth
Spectacular images, what are they worth?

The price of admission is nothing more,
Than to grab a lawn chair, and open the door.

Gather a blanket, call a friend,
Get in your car, this message I send.

Pick a nice place, out on the grass,
I promise you people, you will have a gas!!

Can you guess the show I describe?
Watch it enough, you will feel more alive.

Then ever before, see nature's way,
I know you'll want more, than you can see in one day.

The clouds make some incredible shapes,
Some like faces, some like apes.

Look at that tree, surely a great Oak,
The wind may blow, a hole it will poke,

Inside its large trunk, like a chainsaw at work,
A burly lumberjack, his duties don't shirk.

Cumulous nimbus, or stratified thin,
Never watched a cloud show, where have you been?

A deep blue backdrop, beautiful sky,
No reason to ask, a question like why.

The evaporation of water, rising above,
The science is cool, to watch it I love!

See the horse, galloping overhead and free,
Make sure your sitting, don't skin your knee.

The lovers and couples will spy a large heart,
After seeing this cloud, the kissing may start.

Bring you dog, lassie he'll see!
Got so excited, he just took a pee.

A hand is common appendage to view,
Its god and he may be reaching for you.

To carry you up, into heaven you'll float,
Smooth as calm waters, when your in a huge boat.

The crux of the biscuit is easy to guess,
Get out and live life, watch the TV less.

See Gods creations, gather them in,
Life is so short, to not live it is a sin!

FIRE

A worldly essential, one of the big four,
Wind, water and earth they open the door,

For life to exist, here on big blue,
Higher life forms, and the lower ones too.

Fire breathes life into our world,
When out of control, chaos is hurled.

Still in the cave, discovered by chance,
Lightning hits trees, man took a closer glance.

Thought long ago, that angry gods,
Brought down fire, with staff and rods.

This may hold true, god leads by example,
Once given us fire, life becoming more ample.

Friction can cause heat to appear,
Rubbing two sticks, the answer is clear.

Give it some air, inferno to build,
Don't stand to close, or you will be killed.

Cook our food, stay warm in the cave,
Fire for people, is now all the rave.

Greatness its true, no argument made,
Never extinguished, earns a passing grade.

I think paradoxical, is the word,
Gives and takes life, many have heard,

The bittersweet song that fire doth sing,
Kept warm in the winter, breaths life until spring,

To close to the core of this wondrous thing,
Charred to a crisp, emotions still sting,

Rituals and religion use it to play.
A necessary evil is fire today.

Back to the big four, wind needed to heat,
And continue a fire, without air its beat.

Extinguish a fire, don't pour on it gas!
Earth or water, will destroy all its mass.

Earth, wind, water and fire, there power elite,
Use them properly, the life cycle is complete.

DOGS

Who is the one, that always greets you,
Happy and friendly, in humans so few.

His anatomy differs, from humans for sure,
Yell and scream, he'll come back for more.

Big or small, it matters not,
Panting its tongue, means he's hot.

Tail wagging fiercely, true to his mood,
Loyal and trustworthy, and often times lewd.

He scratches and licks, whenever he please,
These may be signs, of infestation with fleas.

Have you guessed yet, of the species I speak?
A canine of coarse, some scary some meek!

A wolf its thought his ancestors be,
Domestic now, his spirit still free.

Just watch him run and tear out the door,
The outdoors ingrained, they always need more.

Time in the wild, to sniff and run free,
They know the location, of every tree.

Be smart or dumb, it matters not,
Unconditional loyalty is what you've got.

Rich or poor, your dog doesn't care,
Short or tall or what you wear.

They give you love, asking little in return,
Just food and drink, you may treat them stern.

And still a dogs master, is forever his chum,
Even if the master, to his dog is a bum.

We humans with all are gadgets and IQ,
Can't match the canine's ability to be true.

Let's take a lesson, from mans best friend,
Love and loyalty to others, is the message to send.

EARTH

Gases and ice, raw elements do drift,
Floating and waiting, no one to monitor or sift.

Two clouds converge, chemicals mix,
An electric charge added, now impossible to nix.

An enormous explosion, dwarfing man's nuclear fusion,
Light years away, the residents know its no illusion.

The big bang theory comes to fruition,
A new galaxy's creation is the ultimate mission.

Eons pass and the explosions wane,
Stars and comets this galaxy does gain.

Cooling and moving, the Milky Way is born,
Molten hot magma, off stars, planets are torn.

A billion years more, planets orbits due create,
Now the laws of physics can no longer wait.

Solar systems split, let's visit Sol,
A star on the arm of the Milky Way pole.

The third planet orbiting around this sun,
We're calling it Earth, its loaded with fun.

Green grass and water, oxygen atmosphere,
Carbon based life grows, and it's getting clear,

A special place is this planet Earth,
Lush and fertile, always showing her worth.

Home of many species, humans just one,
Dominance they claim, their time may be done.

BEACHES

Get to the water, no matter the work,
Good feelings for you, and many other perk.

Primal is the need, to see water swell,
Listen to the sound, take in the smell.

Watch the surfers, catching a ride,
He's hanging ten, a walk on the wild side!

Look at that guy, buried in the sand,
Can't move a muscle, or wiggle his hand.

A child builds a castle, helped by his dad,
A hallmark moment is what you just had.

Float in the water on a rubber raft,
Its therapeutic, don't think that I'm daft!

See the umbrellas symmetrically aligned,
Walk in between them, a friend you may find.

Stroll on the beach, the sand between your toes,
I promise it will melt away your woes.

See the children gathering shell,
You on your knees, collecting as well.

Lay in the sun, grab all the rays,
Fun it abounds, in so many ways.

Place on sun block, protecting the skin,
A day on the beach, you surely will win!

MANKIND

Mankind crawled years ago out of the sea,
Bearing no resemblance to you or me.

The earth was hot, lush and green,
Dinosaurs abound, really quite a scene.

Crawling on the ground, on all fours,
Too soon erect, and walking through doors.

Live in the cave, sturdy and strong,
Mankind's first home, a community did belong,

Inside its walls, procreation increased,
Smarter we got than Earth's other beast.

Using our grey matter to invent and create,
New ways to hunt and put food on our plate.

Planting seeds and watch them grow,
Plenty to eat, even when there is snow,

Upon the ground, learning to save,
And store our supplies, new needs we do crave.

The arts will soon flourish, start with cave walls,
Music and singing, the mind always calls,

For new better things to enjoy life's way,
Enhance our humanity, free time to play.

Walk out of the cave, it served us well,
Building a house, with a push button bell.

Humans still striving to achieve, we want more!
Building wooden ships, the planet to explore.

Settle new continents, continue to flow,
The population expanding, watching it grow.

Birthing many great minds, like Einstein and the Bard,
Finding resources is no longer is hard.

Landing on the moon, new horizons do call,
Ships no longer wood, now titanium's the wall,

Will carry humanity out into space,
Help plant human DNA to another place!

DISEASE

The last fifty years, progress has been made,
In the sod people are older, when they're laid.

Infections on the run, bacteria in fear,
Every decade that passes, lifespan adds another year.

What of the virus, humans living in fear,
Science will win, life we cherish too dear.

Plasmid replication, viral loads will reduce,
These new medications may come from a spruce.

Cancer treatments more effective every day,
People getting well, humans always find a way.

Smarter are people, than ever before,
Changing behaviors, have opened the door.

To a long and happy life, free from disease,
This enhancement has a price, not coming with ease.

Many folks have died, many tears have been shed,
In the hope that loved ones will never be dead.

These emotions and longing and the thirst for life,
Wanting one more day, with your parents or wife,

Will keep the fire burning, in our immortal soul,
To enhance the humananity, never accepting the hole,

That is waiting for every man women and child,
No I say! Let science go wild!

Recombinant DNA, organs to clone,
Send back the reaper, create a new bone.

Spend money used now for bullets and war,
To extend human life, of years I want more.

This marvel of science will bind countries together,
No more bombs or disease, no matter what the weather.

It may take some time, but I have no doubt,
Mankind comes together, hear the people shout.

Heaven is on Earth, endless is our life,
No longer is there disease, no longer is there strife.

EMOTIONS

Human emotions help keep us alive,
In ancient times they inspired us to thrive.

The fear of starvation made Neanderthals rough.
It decreases reaction time, so hunting's less tough.

Fear greatly enhances all the physical senses,
Fight or flight reactions help men hurdle fences.

Adrenalin secretion will get your heart pumping,
Muscles contracting, on the ground feet are thumping.

Cortisol is released for an intense energy burst,
Thoughts of food are decreased, and so is your thirst.

Anger creates a response similar to fear,
When properly controlled, many hold it quite dear.

Don't lash out at what's getting under your skin,
Channel your anger, it may help you win.

Sports incorporate this emotional change,
Maneuvering anger, increases athletic range.

Many great competitors are often upset,
Air Jordon on the court, was always beset.

His prowess lied in the ferocity of his attack,
Both physical and mental, his will never did crack.

Passion is the mental state that I cherish the most,
It can lead you to prominence, in your mind you may host,

Thoughts of greatness, increase the knowledge of man,
Break records, curing disease, increase our life span.

Passion is vital, for humanity's ultimate survival,
Caring about advancement has no worthy rival.

Passion for a women, your family or a child,
Keeps living spicy, never getting mild.

Emotions are paramount, for a long healthy life,
Hundreds occur daily, for people, a career or your wife.

LOVE

There are four worldly possessions, big blue holds dear,
Earth, wind, water and fire, we give them a cheer.

A fifth resource makes it all clear,
Shared by many, we need it to steer,

Love is the element, of which I speak,
Not found in the periodic chart, but without it life's bleak.

Fueling of the heart, love breaths into it life,
Not just for a women, you call her your wife.

But of nature and mankind, every year you're around,
Listen closely, hear the sweet sound.

It calls your name, and you must comply,
Without its embrace, you surely will die.

You see love in every country on earth,
Charity feeding the hungry, and earning their worth.

Oil is spilled, wild life in trouble,
Man washing a duck, and the soap makes a bubble.

Think about this wonderful scene,
Now smile to yourself, its pretty keen.

Love its seen not just in people,
Get too close to a nest, perched high on a steeple,

Mother bird attacks you, protecting her young,
Gives her life, that their bodies are flung,

Into the blue younder, generations survive,
Love is given and received, by ever thing alive!

SATAN

Beelzebub is just one name,
What they stand for is all the same.

Cast out of heaven for not following the rules,
The bowels of the universe, molten lava for pools.

How does it feel to burn night and day,
Or is freezing cold, truly hells way.

Are you alone, I would say no,
But short of souls, definitely so.

God gives his children the chance to repent,
Until the last moment, the reaper is sent.

I'm sure you throw parties, good times do abound,
But never again to hear harps sweet sound.

It may be a sin, but I pity your soul,
Only you have the power and total control.

Over dank dark places, no one wants to live,
Why not ask god, to look fast and forgive.

He is a great being, full of wisdom and is just,
Forget all the struggles, in the past they are dust.

Let him know over is the war,
Souls you'll release, and torture no more.

Pray for forgiveness, I know he will hear,
It may take a while, even several year.

But god loves all his flock, and Satan its true,
Scream to the heavens, and no more are you blue.

MISTAKES

We all are imperfect, shared with every Earthly creature,
Making mistakes, is our only common feature.

Not just people are caught making poor choices,
Prey not seeing predator, then silenced are their voices.

A rabbit attempting, escape from a hawk,
Ran in the wrong direction, now his bones used as chalk.

Humans have made many gigantic mistake,
Toxic waste dumped, and destroying a lake.

A man tempted by a young and sweet beauty,
The wife won't know, this girl's a real cutie.

The marriage destroyed, when the cutie found out,
The man was using her, to the wife she did shout.

The atom bomb dropped on an occupied city,
Only years down the road, humans knew this not witty.

What I'm saying is clear, there's no escape to be found,
Mistakes define us, when we hear the bitter sound.

Trying always to live with the consequences we've met,
Due to poor choices, you must never forget,

Mistakes have a lesson, please examine and find,
The message is there, to help enhance your mind.

Don't repeat a mistake, learn from bad calls,
Avoid tripping again, and having hard fall!

SANDY

The sky grew dark, and the wind blew around,
Electricity cables fell to the ground.

Trees started falling, devastation in store,
Affected us all, both rich and the poor.

Roadways are blocked, in the wake of her ire;
Firemen try desperately, to put out a fire.

The storm named Sandy, hit land today,
Death and destruction, in her wake they lay.

Tunnels flooded, railways failed,
People of New York feel like there jailed.

Plains and trains and roads are taboo,
Canned goods only, no power to make stew.

Driving around is ugly, and sad,
The real loss of hope is people, there bad.

The gas station has a very long line,
Brace for the worst, for TV they do pine.

Two men cursing, and then came their fist,
They snared at each other, like snakes they both hissed.

Why did the fight start, I heard some say,
He cut the line, and got in my way.

A coffee shop opens, with power to cook,
Hard turn off the road, people don't even look,

Where they drive, now an accident to clear,
Needs to be met, no lives they hold dear.

When nightfall comes, the thieves start their work,
No power or alarms, tonight we won't shirk.

Looting and pillage, the city is ours,
No emergency phone, down are cell towers.

This horrible story has a happy end,
Folks working together, good cheer they do send.

Clearing roads, electricity restored,
Cutting down trees, cement is re-poured.

Surviving Sandy, together we work,
Overcoming adversity, not being a jerk.

The human condition is thriving and well,
It takes an emergency, to ring the bell,

Getting each other to be at their best,
A love of each other, never failing the test.

CHAPTER 4
HISTORIC POEMS

HOLIDAYS

Glad you enjoyed, your family time,
Celebration, drinks made with lime.

I know that holidays can be a drag,
Family arguments, they pick and nag,

And bring you down, when up you should be,
It's what you make it, don't you agree?

Sisters, brothers, and in-laws must fight,
Retaining their position, maintaining family height.

Not wanting to give their power away,
Let's go there for coffee, not long we need stay.

Needn't wait for holidays, to bring happiness and cheer,
Visit any day of the week, with family have a beer.

Tell them what they mean to you, without hesitation or fear,
Their first response is hugging you, telling you to come near.

But people have their stupid pride,
They get behind it, we all must hide.

To many people, family relations do get lost,
This comes to some at a terrible cost.

The family members, most dear, meaning to you the most,
I think you won't understand, till one of them is a ghost.

VALENTINE

The day is filled with loving and song,
Professing that feelings are powerfully strong.

Literature is written and libraries are packed,
With tales of passion, that cities were sacked.

For the love of a women, kings brought to a knee,
Waiting for a sight, he's longing to see.

Imploded are lungs, the air is sucked out,
When the sight of her face is showing some doubt.

She isn't sure that you are the one,
Giving her heart and with others be done.

So pick a day that's dreary and cold,
To profess your feelings, be totally bold.

Dinner reservations and chocolate candy,
Keep a dozen roses easily handy.

Gift wrap a present and tape on a bow,
Surely these gifts will make her love grow.

Valentine's day is only a token,
A reflection of words, that need to be spoken,

Every day, make your lady aware,
You love and adore her, show her you care.

Take her not for granted, compliment and say,
You really are looking beautiful today.

Never miss a chance to impress your girl,
You like her new perfume or the hair that has curl.

Make love often, even when you are tired,
Pillow talk with her after you've sired.

Look at her each time, as though its the first,
Show her emotions, let them all burst.

Follow these tips and she'll be at your side,
Always being your friend, your life helping to guide.

EASTER

Easter time is for rejoicing, dead and risen,
Not just Jesus, but those stuck in prison.

Actual bars, or self made prison, we all bear a cross,
Jesus died on it, and was laid in the moss.

When bereaved friends came, to visit and cry,
What they would see would shock their eye.

Not just their eyes, but the whole worlds too,
Jesus was gone, body and soul had flew.

What's left was a rag, they had placed on his face,
He had died without money, a cave was his place.

And risen he did, way up on a cloud,
While angry at man, of his son God was proud.

The death of Jesus, is a symbol of life,
When we leave this world, with the pain and the strife,

So to our soul it will rise, and take wing,
And to the feet of God, will fly and bring,

The final judgment, from way up above,
Don't be afraid, he is only pure love.

He won't judge you too harshly, his word is of hope,
Go to him quickly, take flight and don't mope.

The creator and his son are waiting our return,
Of his name and his word, many people do spurn.

Science can explain, both of heaven and the earth,
Still I wonder about those, dose it diminish their worth?

When they spread the word of evolution and the ape,
Does God get upset, that his children should rape,

His actions and good judgment, and try to explain,
That there is no God, this must cause him great pain.

FIREWORKS

Civilized mankind has a unique way,
To party and celebrate a most special day.

Potassium and sulfur, mixed with some coal,
Can reduce a mountain into the hill of a mole.

Gunpowder is thought to have China as a start,
Ceremonies commence, fireworks a part.

I always thought, it amusing to find,
Warfare and festival are two of a kind.

Powerful explosions that disable and destroy,
Have the ability to give the masses such joy.

Here we go, let the bash begin,
Guaranteed to give, your face a grin.

Let's add some luminosity to this summer blast,
Firecrackers and sparklers make the jubilee last.

Pinwheels are nailed safely to a tree,
Furiously twirls colors for all to see.

An aerial assault aloft, hear them roar,
Yellows and greens, in the air they will soar.

Flash flaming fluorescence, blue and red,
Envelop your eyes, dancing in your head.

See the trail of a missile, zipping in flight,
Shiny illuminations, all through the night.

On the ground at the end of a fireworks show,
Blazing stars and stripes, a flag created, watch it glow.

The fourth of July is America's time,
A birthday blowout, drinks with lemon and lime.

This frolicking is filled with food, family and fun,
Independence day, I wish it never was done.

HALLOWEEN

The sun is setting in the west,
Birds are sleeping in their nest.

The darkness comes, the stars are out,
The Earth's natural satellite makes me shout!

Full moon tonight, the time is right,
For goblins to come a calling.
This may seem trite, great strength tonight,
Jump on you and you'll be falling.

A full moon you say, is the werewolf's day,
A silver bullet you need.
Howling with delight, the beast is quite a sight,
Fire quick, he has amazing speed.

The witches brew, children in the stew,
There flesh as sweet as molasses.
Eye of newt, its not real cute,
Make sure you hide their glasses!

The man with a cape, his fangs they will gape,
A large vein in your neck.
If he drains you dry, your relations may cry,
Now you're immortal, what the heck!

Its Halloween, let's make a scene,
I love all this scary stuff,
Legends they be, can't hurt you or me,
Don't be so sure its a bluff!

THANKSGIVING

Come to this land, thought it was grand,
Pilgrims cross the Atlantic,
Starving and cold, weather was bold,
They found the place gigantic.

Devastation is near, the Indians fear,
Their neighbors may not survive,
Open their heart, planting they start,
Food to keep them alive.

Emergency done, the neighbors had fun,
A vast alliance was born.
Trading techniques, farming it keeps,
Growing a staple called corn

Harvest complete, grabbing a seat,
They broke some bread together.
The table was long, built firm and strong,
Colder was getting the weather.

Sharing a feast, turkey the beast,
And many favorite dishes.
The meal was fine, sharing some wine,
Nothing but love and good wishes.

This was the first, eat till you burst,
An American holiday tradition.
Offer thanks for the bounty, in every American county,
A dream has come to fruition.

CHRISTMAS

Bows and ribbons placed on gifts,
Uplifting holiday, your spirit it lifts.

Another birthday celebration with cake and candle,
Depression rates high, holidays are hard to handle.

Family and friends like to get together,
Tends to be cold, beware snowy weather.

Drinking some cheer and eating your feast,
Stuffing with side dishes, turkey the beast.

Trimming a tree and placing lights on the house,
Not a creature is stirring, not even a mouse.

Saint Nick is coming, he lands on the roof,
Slides down the chimney then suddenly poof!

Presents are stacked, up high as can be,
Barely can see the lights on the tree.

Santa has eaten the cookies, and drained all the milk,
Mom got diamond earrings, and a dress made of silk.

This sounds like a scene, from a Rockwell play,
Easy to loose sight, of what were celebrating today.

The birth of the greatest man on the Earth,
Read the Bible, miracles show his real worth,

Worried and cared about every living soul,
Love and good wishes he did easily dole.

Born in poverty, his first bed was a manger,
In thirty three years he would be in real danger.

Those years he spent, spreading the word of God,
Be of good faith, before your laid under the sod.

Love and cherish each other, and this place,
Ascending into heaven, sharing my fathers space.

Everybody enjoy Christmas, a great time of the year,
Happy birthday to Jesus, his spirit is still here!

GLUE

Go slow baby, and take lots of time,
The family needs you to draw a straight line.

Help work out problems, some may seem small,
You must be strong and give it your all.

Tired and down, who cares about you?
Give me a chance to take in the view.

Your older and wiser, help keeping them true,
Listen and understanding, chase away their mood blue.

Now that mom is no longer there,
You're the strong women, take control if you dare.

I've learned a hard lesson from the death of my mom,
Women hold families together, without them a bomb,

Will fall from the rooftop, destroying the root,
That sweet mother planted, the men they all loot,

And plunder and scurry, caring only for self,
No thought to the family, and the state of it's health.

Give of your self and help keep it going,
The family it needs you, your mom she is knowing,

The work and the love that she placed in you,
Will bloom and blossom, and carry family through.

These difficult times you'll never forget,
Mom always with you, of that you can bet.

She's watching and praying and sending her love,
You see it daily in the sunrise above.

So listen to me and heed all my verse,
Without a strong women, family health will get worse.

Women are the glue that keeps families together,
Rain or shine, no matter what the weather.

FAMILY

In the core of an apple, you find many seed,
These things are responsible, for filling a need.

The need I speak of is procreation, and the ability to grow,
The core of humans is the family, of this I think you know.

The human family is essential to survive,
Its cohesiveness and structure, helps keep us alive.

As an embryo in utero, just a seed yourself,
The family will nurture, and help give you wealth.

The wealth that I speak of, has many different form,
Protection from danger, like the wrath of a storm.

Predators that come, have many different disguise,
Are seen by the family, with most discerning eyes.

Protect and keep safe, from the predators grasp,
Tightly knit is the family, can't penetrate its clasp.

Wisdom and caring, hold the key,
To family survival, for you and me.

The heart of this group, are elders for sure,
They've laid the foundation, the cement they pour.

Sets the foundation, for family to grow,
Unfortunately, western culture just sees them as just slow.

And not important, there mind is not clear,
Even in there own house, no one will hear.

What is said by the elder, there opinion doesn't count,
The studies are in, and the evidence mounts,

The more generations, living under one roof,
The family more solid, members less likely to goof,

By committing some wrong, to others by chance,
Having family around, helps members take a stance.

To help protect one another, keeping loved ones sound,
Always someone there, to keep feet on the ground

The youth benefit from what the family doth bring,
Some families tell jokes, other learn to sing.

Nurture and coddle, teach youth to fly,
Setting up rules, to live your life by.

Encourage and wisdom is not always there,
When the family is nuclear, nobody around to care.

Mom and dad hard working they be,
Can't monitor their children, don't always see.

What goes on after school, between 3 and 6,
Becomes easy to get, caught up in the mix.

Of lost children, sex, drugs or they steal,
Break into a car, with the law they will deal.

Let's maintain the family, honor kin folk,
Respect their rituals, no fun at them poke.

Watch the children, parents get involved,
Do these things, Americas' problems will be solved.

DILEMMA

I sit here feeling light headed and sick,
The cloud in my head, heavy and thick.

There comes to all, a moment of plight,
That supersedes both wrong and right.

A dilemma may at anytime come,
Wipes out families, leaving barely a crumb.

They come in many, ominous forms,
Earthquakes, fires, and terrible storms.

You read about them in the papers,
Young man in a car, crushed like a wafer.

Or a young women caught in a raging flood,
Her body found downstream, devoid of blood.

Be not quick to judge that man on the news,
That killed himself in church by the pews.

These acts may seem, heartless and cold,
And extremely scary and totally bold.

The dilemma they faced was totally real,
And stole from them there power to deal,

With any and all of the crisis at hand,
Powers of reason, buried deep in the sand.

He jumped to his death and his final wish,
Was his cremated ashes placed in a dish.

DOORS

Turn the knob and walk right through,
Opportunity is waiting, have you a clue?

Stasis is desired, revision is hard,
Diet and exercise, loosing some lard.

Start a new career, causes many a fright,
Days fearing error, sleepless is their night.

But facing the things that make you drip sweat,
Enhance your worth, once the challenge is met.

It matters not if you succeed or fail,
Try new things, refuse to get stale.

Patterns are comfortable, most dislike change,
Open your mind, expanding your range.

Enhance all experiences, take comfort and caress,
The wonder of variance, refuse to regress.

Forge on and accomplish another new task,
Take time and enjoy, in new achievements to bask.

Surprised are you, flexibility keeps us alive,
Ruling the Earth, not just wanting to survive.

Humans must modify, history reports,
Things done differently, unexplainable torts.

Progress is the key, behavior not always just,
The goal is the same, enhancement a must!

FENCES

The Western world has got a thing,
About marking Earth, a fence they bring.

A governmental agency, with records they keep,
So the taxes are paid, they certainly are steep.

Fences separate us from our next door neighbor,
Work only on your plot, expend no more labor.

Trapping your dog, make sure their contained,
Work hard on the lawn, your energy it has drained.

Not only homeowners are big on a fence,
Countries use it, makes very little sense.

Cutting them off from a potential friend,
What kind of message does this send?

Manifests an attitude of mistrust and unrest,
Be nice to your neighbor, treat them the best!

When mankind rips down fences all around the world,
An new age will dawn, into peace we are hurled.

Combining our resources, working hard together,
Understanding our neighbors, moods light as a feather.

This does occasionally happen, let's take a look,
When disaster strikes, people break out the hook.

And pull together, the world a unified force,
Helping effected areas, to get back on course.

Why can't this happen on a regular basis?
The world making progress, instead of in stasis.

Listen to me, there are no more fences aloud,
Love all your neighbors, and make them feel proud.

CHAPTER 5
PATRIOTIC POEMS

911

Look up in the sky, planes flying low,
Crashing into buildings, not where they should go.

Pilot error it was thought, during crash number one,
Then a second collision, made the people run.

New York under siege, an attack by the air,
The snake named Bin Laden, who else would dare?

The trade towers stood for many a year,
At the world's financial center, did terrorists leer.

The world watched, as the towers came down,
A huge white cloud, and a thunderous sound.

The finest and the bravest, lost their lives,
Calls made to the husbands and the wives,

We have bad news, your love one has died,
Out of the rubble, their body was plied.

There life it ended, in towers one or two,
Many lives ended that day, others were just through.

What of the workers, looking through the rubble,
Years down the road, the death toll would double.

From sickness and disease, contracted at ground zero,
Families can't survive on the memory of a hero.

Many years have passed, freedom tower erected,
People stay sharp, terror must be detected.

And wiped out completely, US leads the way,
But for now on your knees, and everybody pray,
For the souls we lost on that frightful day,

Ask God to relieve, the pain that day brought,
Renew peoples hope, give direction if sought.

FLAG

I may be prejudiced, an American I be,
Our flag looks the best, take a gander and see.

Red white and blue, these colors don't fade,
Betsy Ross sowed the first one made.

A hundred other flags fly at the UN,
Soldiers leave as boys, and come home as men.

One stripes for each original state,
13 in all, our country is great!

50 states now, each is shown by a star,
Look at a map, rediscover where they are.

The flag first made by Ms. Ross,
In the Smithsonian, not a total loss,

Originally hung over staunch battle field,
Bombs exploding all around, still it would not yield.

Many holes in the middle and burnt on the edge,
When visiting the museum, allegiance I will pledge.

Still some folk like to target our flag,
Stomp and burn, I think it's a drag,

We send monies and help reduce,
Fatalities from famine, can't they deduce.

We're here to help the country to grow,
Opposing the help, how little they know.

The flag is flying in many other land,
Protecting our neighbor and his right to their sand.

Our flag on every continent on the Earth,
Protecting democracy, enhancing our worth.

FORCES

Let's all give a great big cheer,
Please give thanks, and hold them dear.

They fly, swim, and walk the earth,
To others and us, invaluable their worth.

I'm talking about the Service Corp.
Fighting our battles, and so much more.

Army engineers drain New York City,
After Sandy, Manhattan wasn't pretty.

The Marine Corp. standing varies post,
Like in Penn Station, embrace them the most.

The men and women in uniform dress,
Protect us from ruins, clean up the mess.

That other governments leave in the dust,
Protection from dictators, their survival a must.

The Navy patrolling the vast seven seas,
Without them, we surely would be on our knees.

From attacking countries, too many to count,
The need for strength continues to mount.

The Air Force flying high in the sky,
Daily trip to Alaska, Russia is why.

Intel they give us, of threats to our land,
Protection and safety, the country kept grand.

The British were the first, to feel American wrath,
Succession from England, get out of our path!

Proclamations and orders, we would not obey,
Taxation without representation, no we won't pay!

Washington and the Minute men felled the giant,
Never again would we be compliant.

The Germans and the Kaiser, the next would be,
A huge great threat, to you and me.

Hitler and Mussolini, allied with the Japs,
Thinned out our forces, for many played taps.

The desert wars, starting out with Storm,
Weren't like others, out of the norm.

But just as vital as others we fought,
Ask victims of 911, Hussein he brought.

A new kind of warfare, our forces must contain,
They have blown up the towers, with several plane!

Forces found the snake, that threatens our land,
Now his body is buried, in a grave under the sand.

America prevailed, triumphant, we won,
Always on guard, forces work is never done.

ASSASSIN

Born a human, innocent and young,
Night time his mother's voice has sung,

Sweet melodic songs learned in her youth,
What career would he chose, doctor, lawyer or sleuth?

Uncle Sam made this choice, against mothers will,
Drafted and trained, they taught him to kill.

Gunpowder and death, are the scents in the air,
Many miles away from mom's love and her care.

Common is this scene, man is weaned on war,
Happy is the day the fighting is no more.

But not this day, the bullets fly,
Bombs explode, and men will die.

Special forces have trained this boy well,
His future is set, his mind placed in hell.

Countless incursions behind the enemies line,
An Assassins life is always in a bind.

Given a target, nothing else in his head,
I can't go back, until my mark is dead.

His time in the service has come to an end,
Many targets erased, on a plane they will send,

Him back to mother, innocent no more,
A dark dank distance, for mom is in store.

For many like him, the story ends here,
Lost and alone, his nights filled with fear.

But not the special forces, a letter will be sent,
An opportunity awaits, that will pay all the rent.

We have a position, and qualified you are,
Your records from the service, indicate you were a star.

Come to Washington, see if the jobs OK,
The letters return address, was marked CIA.

WAR

Young men are taken, barely out of the crib,
Sent off to fight, he may fracture a rib,

Or maybe more, much anatomy to loose,
A telegram from Sam, parents no longer snooze.

Cause their young son, mom held in the womb,
Now making plans, for his mortal tomb.

How can this happen? What is this war?
Plenty to bereave, there will always be more.

War is a constant, thousands we've seen,
You'd think by now, humans could wean,

Themselves from the blood lust, a horrible scene,
To each other, people never serene.

The planet is host, many species reside,
Only humans prey on themselves, nowhere to hide.

From the death and destruction, brought on by war,
Government cares not, they will shut the door,

On the troubles and fears, that any war bring,
Come on take a stand, let your lungs sing.

Stop killing our children, and destroying the lands,
People rule the politicians, they are merely our hands.

The masses should decide about national defense,
Tell the government, stop being so dense.

About oil and waterways, and favors we do,
That's why we fight, no lies, this is true.

That bullets and bombs kill and they maim,
On the orders of a dignitary, you don't know his name.

He has done us a favor, our country in debt,
Kill all his rivals, of this you can bet.

Children will be damaged, for reasons unknown,
Screaming and pain, a guttural moan.

From the injured and dying, our soldiers, they fight,
Thinking what they do, protects us from plight.

The truth be known, many die or are hurt,
From a foreign blue blood, his words they are curt,

To keep his good graces, our leaders they fear,
Noncompliance will raise oil prices this year.

Untold resources are squandered away,
Both human and natural, when war is in play.

Of the young dead bodies, lawmakers don't die,
Nor do their children, they never will cry.

Safe and secure, there children in schools,
It's the common folk, these vipers make fools.

Why must we break, Gods golden rule,
And treat your com padre, like a pile of stool.

Start loving your neighbor, like you love your self,
If we lived by this rule, more emotional wealth,

Would be in our lives, war is now dead,
No more would parents, need to dread.

The loss of there children, both boy and girl,
Stop the tornado, be still its strong swirl.

Love one another, be kind and do trust,
To survive as a species, these words are a must!

KENT

The times had unrest, civil authority was uptight,
Police plotting and scheming, all through the night.

The problem was that times were beginning to change,
Boundaries placed on the government, their power had less range.

The mothers and fathers didn't understand why,
Children right out of high school, were sent off to die.

This wasn't like past days, when dictators were a threat,
Acceptable were those losses, world order was reset.

The last two wars were unpopular by far,
A cold war has tarnished the American star.

So people started shouting, voices loud and be strong,
Protestors carried signs, and their numbers were getting long.

Colleges were the sites where students complained the most,
In 1970 at Kent State, a protest they did host.

The college administrators alarmed by it's size,
Called in the police, they were scared by the cries,

Of end Vietnam, what's the purpose of this campaign?
End the death and disability, this war is insane!

The National Guard was put on alert,
The uniforms crisp, no intention to hurt.

Things got out of hand, and guns did unleash,
Orders from a man, who advanced on a beach,

During World War II, but things are different today,
Killing American citizens is never the way.

Four students in the crowd were murdered that day,
Big news in the papers, but no one would pay.

Miller, Krause, Scheuer and Schroeder, didn't deserve this fate,
Narrow minded thinking is loaded with fear and with hate.

These four should be heroes, Arlington cemetery the place,
Forever remembered, held in the highest grace.

VIETNAM

Way back to the sixties, a time of civil unrest,
America was changing, new ideas we would test.

Self-expression, was a popular trait,
Divorce increasing, find a new mate.

War was raging, some things don't change,
Young men were dying, in the 19-year-old range.

The voice of the people, was trying to be heard,
Protests and rallies, politicians fear the word.

The message that the masses did send,
Stop all the killing, relations to mend.

The old regime wasn't going down easy,
Our leaders harbored secrets, many quite sleazy.

The press and the media were getting very strong,
Exposing many details, liars not lasting very long.

Strong were demonstrations, bullets flying at Kent,
The Guard killing four, the voters getting bent.

The President impeached, lying to the crowd,
Speeches by Nixon, the boos getting loud.

Pardoned by the President, averted was a scandal,
Many years of media hype, all they could handle.

The draft has ended, also the war in Vietnam,
Fifty thousand dead, by those dropping a bomb,

What of the Vietcong? We never hear their numbers,
Of dead, or the villages killed, and put to fiery slumber.

Its not clear why we fought this war,
The fabric of Americana forever shall be tore.

TERRORISM

People held hostage, always living in fear,
The barrel of a weapon is always near.

Riding the train, a skin curdling scream,
A deafening noise and a sharp light beam.

A violent shock wave tears open your flesh,
The lucky ones receive skin grafts with mesh.

Your arm torn off, artery bleeding is profuse,
A dying thought is what was the use?

What was the purpose, to kill all these people?
In the name of Allah, perched on a mosque steeple.

Radical extremists don't care about life,
Just murder people, and increase human strife.

Wasting resources, bringing the Earth gloom,
Look at faces on a plane, many filled with doom.

The last thirty-five years I don't understand,
Middle Eastern countries, together they band.

Bringing terror and hatred towards cultures of the west,
We accept the need to feel your ways are the best.

Pray all you like, cover up a women's face,
Stop trying to change America's philosophy and place.

Once the oil is gone, and the land again bare,
Back to living in tents, flowing robes you will wear.

Your tactics are old, soon you may feel,
The burning of flesh, this inferno is real.

A nuclear explosion will end years of frustration,
No longer putting up with terrorist's indignation.

Revolutions reveal, the world ending in flame,
Enough with this nonsense, put an end to this game.

CARS

America is large, with much flat land,
The perfect landscape, to maneuver with one hand.

When first discussed, with the powers that be,
Attempting to finance, sheer folly, show me.

Mr. Ford why place capital with you,
Funds are short, and it sounds untrue.

How it will move, what power source?
No muscles working, what to come of the horse?

Like all great inventions, it was met with scorn,
And like many great men, in poverty he was born.

The automobile was well on its way,
To worldwide use, hear the people say,

Look at its lines, and pretty curves,
It handles the road, Oh how it swerves!

The ford plant was started, and soon on its way,
To stimulate economies, and create jobs that would stay,

For a hundred years, and maybe more,
Fords assembly line opened the door.

For the steel and tire plants, production was good,
Let's open this hatch, and peer under the hood!

Look at the engine, explosions inside,
Controlled and in unison, that make the wheels ride.

Gears that help, make the car move,
Shifting them can make a man groove.

Add lights and a roof, more time to spend,
Inside its beauty, the message will send.

The Auto can make the country great,
For goods and supplies, we need not wait.

A variation of the car, the truck was made,
Moving mountains of products, it sure made the grade.

An infrastructure is needed, let's pave the land,
Construction is booming, to cover the sand,

And make the way, for the car to take,
People away, from the home they make.

And visit others, living far away,
Called a vacation, at a hotel we can stay.

Without further delay, I could explain,
The auto's workings, with detail and with pain.

So instead of the detail, it suffices to say,
The auto revolutionized our world in this way:

Making commuting to work, from far away,
An easier trip, in the suburbs we lay.

The beach and the mountains, easy to see,
Hotels and new towns, into existence they be.

More fun into life, leisure time will be added,
The nations economy will be largely padded.

The innovation of the car, is not only grand,
It has forced mother earth, to take a harsh stand.

Climatic changes, and temperatures rise,
Greenhouse gases, are these things wise?

Will the planet survive? Humans in peril,
Poisons and toxins, may cause us to be sterile.

Disease and death, like cancerous lung,
Bittersweet is the song, the car has sung.

Make your decision, please choose a side,
Either walk with your feet, or get in and ride.

HOLLYWOOD

The magic of the silver screen has been around so long,
Starting out in silence, films soon would have song.

Dancing too up on the screen, Gene Kelly made his mark,
Watch him spin around the stage, or dancing in the park.

Love film and World War II, Bogart was the star,
He and Bergman in Casablanca, fans from near and far.

"Play it again Sam", a famous line, known by many folk,
Germans threaten to rule the world, subject matter was no joke.

The Civil war, the setting was, for the next great flick,
Rhett Butler and his girl Scarlet, always a great pick.

"Frankly my dear, I don't give a damn", was the famous line,
75 years young today, this picture still is fine.

A film about family life, a 1947 prize,
Jimmy Stewart stayed at home, Bedford Falls, just his size.

Clarence heard a bell, and he did earn his wings,
He helped poor George, win back his life, and many other things.

Enter Eastwood and the western, America likes it rough.
John Wayne was the first rope slinger, 4 star pictures he has enough.

I love to watch hang 'em high, one of Eastwoods best,
Been around for 40 years, I think it's passed the test.

Comedy has been a theme, to split your sides with joke,
Abbot always hitting Costello, and with his fingers poke.

Hope, Goodman and George burns too, laughing in your seat.
See them all in Technicolor, really quite a treat!

Just a few that entertain, and make our play time fun,
More to come, the actor's guild, never will be done.

SCREEN

When last we met, the story read of pictures that were old,
They laid the bricks for more movies, Their story line so bold.

We last left off with comedies, so here is were we'll start,
Hoffman in a tight red dress, soap actor was his part.

Tootsie is a classic flick, its famous near and far,
It's younger than the Graduate, that part made him a star.

Many men in Hollywood have put on them a dress,
Robin Williams in Mrs. Doudtfire, brilliant, nothing less.

His voices and an amazing wit, comedy he does rule,
Williams, Lang and Mcbeal, made Hackman out the fool!

Dramatic roles by Hollywood, many have we seen,
Tom Hanks involved in many fine works, watch him on the screen.

He and Denzel shared the lead, Philadelphia was the play,
A dying lawyer, struck down with AIDS, fired cause he was gay.

Another picture by Mr. Hanks, I think you'll know the name,
Forest Gump, an academy award, the story is not the same.

This poor slow man, runs through history, a tumultuous 30 years,
Powerful stuff, when things get rough, don't listen to your fears.

Stupid is as stupid does, a famous line for sure,
Hanks has won a couple of Oscars, poised he is for more.

So many actors and picture films, I know that I have missed,
Will have to rhyme another poem, make sure I keep a list.

MOVIE

The third of three, the topic is clear, To entertain a must,
Films give immortality, though actors may be dust.

Let's now explore, its all folk law, Celluloid heroes they all be,
Two hours in a movie house, Will set your spirits free!

I haven't touched a genre, very close to my heart,
Science fiction is the theme, effects will play a part,

How you react, did you get scared? Hairs on your neck stand up,
Ever see Kings awesome tale, of a rabid gigantic pup?

Let's move on to outer space, Skywalker is the name,
Blowing up the death star, and causing Vader pain.

Kirk, Spock and Generations, warping into space,
Klingons and the Romulans, they put right in their place!

Let's not forget Arnold, a cyborg he does play,
"I'll be back," is his big line, what terminators say.

Old but good, misunderstood, Rosemarie's baby we will hail,
A covenant of witches, raped by Satan, her baby had a tail,

Aliens are pretty tough, acid is their blood,
Ripley beats them all the time, and turns them into mud.

Predator from outer space, Arnold the star again,
The greatest hunter in the cosmos, not beasts but only men.

The sixth sense, a Willis film, he plays a murdered shrink,
Helps a kid who's seeing ghosts, whenever he should blink.

So there you go, missed some I know, science fiction it is scary,
Don't bring your kids, they'll flip their lids, of dreams you must be wary.

CHAPTER 6
FUN POEMS

RIDING

Hold the clutch, jump up to start,
Shifting weight, enslaving your heart.

Hear it roar, cylinders churn,
Along with the gas, some oil will burn.

Twist the throttle and louder it gets,
The neighbors swear your engines are jets.

Adjust the mirrors, required by law,
Never in use, things you already saw.

Place on a helmet, if the state requires,
Blood is pumping, realize your desires.

Riding a bike is an exhilarating event,
Not for the weak, much energy spent.

Maneuvering the road, enjoying the curves,
A slice of paradise your body deserves.

Many feel that a Harley is king,
Alluring and powerful, a wonderful thing.

Personally, I feel any cycle is great,
Look at the girls, when making a date.

Her eyes a bit wider, a smiling face,
After the ride, into bed you will race.

A bad boy you are, the chicks can't resist,
While cruising the asphalt, pumping your fist!

The world is my oyster, because of my ride,
When dismounting my hog, a little I have died.

JOURNEY

I come from a time, years ago,
Hair was long, some had a fro.

Peace signs were a common site,
During the Vietnam War, emotions were tight.

At the age of fifteen, when school was through,
Bored was I, so I would try something new.

I stuck out my thumb to hitch a ride,
A truck pulled off the road, by my side.

Were you heading partner?" he said with a grin,
Several teeth missing and smelling of Gin.

Out west I think, California way,
Then get right in, I heard him say.

I stayed with him almost a day,
Fast around the curves, sometime I would pray.

His trip ended in the second city,
The end of the line, it sure was pretty.

The tall buildings, and roads by the shore,
I stayed there a while, still the west held allure.

So I bid my new friend a pleasant trip back,
He needed some down time to be in the sack.

Once more on the road, out was my thumb,
What should I hear but a radio hum.

This middle-aged couple pulled over on the shoulder,
Were are you headed, they told me," to Boulder!"

So in I jumped into the muscle car, a '70 GTO,
When he punched the gas pedal, that car would really go!

What are you doing here on the road alone?
I'm taking a trip to California, the wife let out a moan.

Your mother is ok with you out here on the road?
Never let her know, she carries a heavy load.

Not much more said about my time hitching around,
The couple fed me several times, my feet back on the ground.

Here's some cash, please call your home,
Before you leave and further roam.

The journey will continue, I'm fresh out of time,
I will explain the trip more, in my very next rhyme!

JOURNEYS

My journey continues, out on the road,
A red VW bug, off my feet, take a load.

A beautiful girl, a new high school grad,
Moving to Frisco, closer to her dad.

She was going to college at San Jose State,
Promised success, destined to be great.

She never did ask me what was my age,
Where I was going or who was my sage.

Taught me a lesson, I hold dear to this day,
How to make love, and with a women to play.

We pulled that car over at every rest stop,
Never missing an opportunity to thrust and to hop.

Surely, I was sad, when our destination we did reach,
Little did she let me speak or preach.

Good luck sweet Paulie, I had a good day,
Look me up if you need a ride the other way.

Alone on the road, California I'd made,
The scenery was amazing; an "A" was its grade.

I continued to hitch, scoring many rides,
And was picked up by some hippies, a van it hides,

A bag of Mother Nature, we arrived at their commune,
People were kind, and I realized soon,

That free love and fun was plentiful here,
I was smoking herb and drinking a beer.

That night around the bonfire they had built,
The trees started talking and the ground began to tilt.

Some one had slipped me a sugar cube,
With hallucinogenic squeezed from a tube.

Sorry my friends, my time is done,
Tune in next week, to continue the fun!

JOURNEYED

This chapter will complete my 70's trip;
Call me to clarify, many details I did skip.

Living at the commune, farming during the day,
The night was a party, and boy did we play!

Hitching a ride down to Hollywood and Vine,
The City of Angels certainly was fine.

A different life from farming in the Valley,
I met a cute girl whose name was Sally.

She ran away from home, and was working the street,
I gave her some money, for rent and to eat.

Lovemaking was good in her cold water flat,
Sleeping all day, many times we both sat,

Talking and thinking about dreams that we had,
Too much, she would cry and often be sad.

I got to thinking about life back at home,
My parents were worried, no more would I roam.

Low on money, I used Sally's phone,
Called my mom, and listened to her groan.

Please send money, I want to return,
School's starting soon and this year I can't burn.

For days I waited to get hold of the cash,
Western Union stopped my New York dash.

Finally after much time on the street,
Nowhere to sleep and little to eat.

The funding came through; the police were the key,
Helping my parents, get there hands on me.

A greyhound back home, it took almost a week,
Upon returning home, my father would seek,

A proper punishment, guess what he felt?
Many lashes I got on my back with his belt!

Mother was different; she looked in my eye,
Saying little, many tears she did cry.

I'm glad your back home, come give me a hug,
We missed you so much, you big stupid lug!

MONEY

The root of all evil, so it is said,
Pays for bills, even when you're dead.

Because funerals cost very much cash,
To get buried properly, better have a stash.

Back to the living, Semolians pay for the rent,
Greenbacks are worked for, there not heaven sent.

The sweat of your brow, the Zar pays for your car,
And the gas and insurance, that allows you to go far.

The Euro is currency earned by Anglo Saxon folk,
We always need more, it's never a joke,

When the Rubles run short, ask the boss for OT,
A 60 hour work week, no time to spend as we.

But your house will be loaded, with fancy new toys,
Pesos spent on the children, both the girls and the boys.

Sacrifice seeing your children mature,
Earn many Francs, the families not poor.

What most have missed, an alien idea,
Not wildly popular, and fills many with fear,

Is the thought of not keeping up with the crowd,
Spend time with your loved ones, tell them out loud,

Deutsche Marks are not what we are living for,
I give you my time and love that is pure.

We'll have to get buy, without all the new things,
The Lira runs short, I'm sorry if this stings.

If your being a good parent, husband and friend,
It won't matter to them that this message you send.

Just being around, and always having some fun,
Makes up for lost Drachma, its your family that's won.

CHOICES

In the great scheme of life, many choices you make,
Where to work, who to date, your yard when to rake.

The game of hearts is not quite the same,
Who you love and end up with, is all based on aim.

Yes Cupids aim, is sometimes not good,
Dam arrow it lands, in many a strange hood.

Once per chance the target is hit,
They may be charming, attractive and full of wit.

Only the lucky lovers get this type of win,
The arrow is known to bring pain, shame and sin.

Never knowing what's in store for you,
Loving arms and a partner that's totally true,
Or an unfaithful idiot, to make you real blue.

You may think you scored, they look smokin' hot,
Having sex day and night, you love them a lot.

This sounds pretty awesome, is there a down side?
Not unless you count secrets, and the lovers he hides.

The girl that finds sales, and will spend all your cash,
She goes out on black Friday, doing the fifty yard dash.

Coming home the next day, a smile on her face,
I saved money here, and there, and lets not forget that place!

What she fails to tell you, is your fresh out of money,
Say something about it, she'll resign as your honey.

The men are no better, their tempers get hot,
Slobs and the lazy, and the ones that smoke pot.

One time in the game, Cupid seemed to shoot straight,
He gave me a lover, to see I couldn't wait.

We had some good times, but the end is the same,
Bad excuses, feelings hurt, another to tame.

Please freakin' Cupid, have a talk with William Tell,
Take an archery lesson, or your bow I will sell.

You keep making me fall, for the wrong type of mate,
Just want a good friend, not someone to hate.

GIRLS

Did nature make anything more beautiful than a girl?
Silk hair bouncing, the ends have soft curl.

Skin as soft as the pedal of a rose,
Eyes enchanting, never want them to close.

Two lips enticing, watching them move,
Silky red lipstick gets on my groove.

Some women's lips, they like to pout,
When laid upon you, you may want to shout!

Subtle curves, all down the neck,
Smooth and appealing, it makes me a wreck!

Continuing south, we stop at the chest,
Round and firm, I like them the best.

Stand and salute, point towards the sky,
Kissing and fondling can get you real high.

The back and the stomach can be overlooked,
Sleek and shapely, my hands in the nook,

Of her lower back, both seductive and hot,
A little further down, is an erogenous spot.

Her sweet tender box, the ultimate prize,
To kiss and caress, brings tears to my eyes.

Inject into it her prize, throbbing manly delight,
Making love to a woman is a wonderful sight.

Pushing and grinding, the sweat on the ground,
Tape your love making session, a wondrous sound.

The question remains, words soar and they swirl,
Is there beauty on the planet, that compares to a girl?

INTERN

Schooled for years in scientific thought,
Help to save lives is what their taught.

Dissect a cadaver, learn where things fit,
On your feet for hours, never able to sit.

Pre-med has many difficult classes,
Reading anatomy makes you need glasses

You've undergrad degree is just the start,
Graduating med school will take some heart.

Both men and women become doctors these days,
Many specialty fields, some of it pays.

After graduation from medical school,
Better get sleep, soon starts the real gruel.

Thirty-hour days, three days a week,
Your head in a book, at TV don't you peek.

Intern means your first year in the scrubs,
Eating will consist of pizza and subs.

Many get fat and loose muscle tone,
Contact with your family is done by the phone.

Blood and guts and doing scut work,
Never knowing the answers, feeling like a jerk.

Its said the first year is the toughest by far,
No matter how smart, you can't be a star.

Do what the fellow tells you is right,
Drink lots of coffee and stay up all night.

DEATH

Since time begun, man has run,
Always trying to escape.
The reapers grasp, beware his clasp,
If touched your soul will gape.

And take away, your remaining day,
Your spirit now is free,
Do you suppose, he comes to those,
God doesn't want to see?

It seems to me, he has to be,
Taking both saved and damned,
He is no slob, its just his job,
Meet a quota or he'll get jammed.

I do declare, he has no hair,
A skeleton is he,
Dress is black, see only a crack,
His eyes spying thee.

A sickle in hand, not used on land,
Ominous is its sight,
No escape is made, he'll perform a raid,
Soul taken in the night.

Let's make a deal, don't let him steal,
Your precious time to play,
No way to tell, if your going to hell,
His decision you may sway.

Let's put to rest, you cannot test,
His power and his rod,
When it's your time, taken on a dime,
This power comes from God.

Have no fear, the reaper near,
Your time on earth is done.
Go with ease, he aims to please,
Heaven or hell will both be fun!

BLACK

My gal she likes the color black,
She wears it to work, and when on her back.

Most studies show that on a first date,
To pick a bright color will open the gate.

I guess she's not familiar with this work,
When I mentioned the study, I felt like a jerk.

When married most girls choose to wear white,
Not Jo, to her this fashion statement was a plight.

So guess what color for a wedding dress she choose,
That's right, you guessed it, with black panty hose.

When going to work, to black she's a slave,
Her bosses keep thinking I'm dead in the grave.

On the beach she wears black to make her look thin,
I've thrown in the towel, I just can't win.

This fetish with black is not going to pass,
Throw my head in the oven and turn up the gas!!!!!